A Tapestry of Change: Comparative Analysis of the European Color Revolutions

Copyright Page

TITLE: A Tapestry of Change: Comparative Analysis of the European Color Revolutions

1ST Edition

Copyright @ 2023

Roberto M. Rodriguez. All rights reserved.

Table of Contents

A Tapestry of Change: Comparative Analysis of European Color Revolutions

By Roberto Miguel Rodriguez

Chapter 1: The Role of Social Media in the European Color Revolutions

The Rise of Social Media Platforms in Europe

In recent years, the world has witnessed a remarkable transformation in the way social, political, and cultural movements unfold. One significant contributing factor to this change has been the rise of social media platforms. This subchapter explores the role of social media in the European color revolutions, shedding light on the profound impact these platforms had on various aspects of these transformative movements.

The European color revolutions, characterized by widespread protests and demands for political change, were not exempt from the influence of social media. Platforms such as Facebook, Twitter, and YouTube played a pivotal role in mobilizing and organizing protesters, facilitating communication, and disseminating information. This chapter seeks to analyze the ways in which social media platforms were utilized by activists, examining the strategies employed and the challenges faced in harnessing the power of these digital tools.

One aspect worth exploring is the influence of social media on artistic expressions and cultural movements within the European color revolutions. Social media platforms provided artists and cultural activists with a powerful medium to express their dissent and challenge the status quo. This subchapter delves into the ways in which art, music, and cultural movements were able to flourish and resonate on a broader scale through the use of social media.

Furthermore, this section also explores the impact of economic factors on the European color revolutions and how social media played a role in shaping these dynamics. The interconnectedness of social media platforms allowed for the rapid dissemination of economic grievances and exposed corruption and economic inequality. This chapter investigates how social media influenced the economic demands of protesters and how economic factors shaped the trajectory of these revolutionary movements.

Additionally, the subchapter examines the gender dynamics and feminism within the European color revolutions, focusing on how social media platforms provided a platform for feminist voices and movements. It analyzes the ways in which social media facilitated the mobilization and organization of feminist protests, as well as the challenges faced by women activists in these movements.

Overall, this subchapter emphasizes the significance of social media platforms in the European color revolutions, showcasing their impact on various aspects such as artistic expressions, economic factors, gender dynamics, and more. By understanding the role of social media in these transformative movements, historians can gain a deeper understanding of the complexities and long-term effects of the European color revolutions on European politics.

Utilizing Social Media for Mobilization and Organization

In the digital age, social media has become a powerful tool for mobilization and organization in various social and political movements. The European color revolutions, which took place during the early 2000s, were no exception. This subchapter explores the role of social media in these revolutions and how it facilitated mobilization and organization.

Social media platforms such as Facebook, Twitter, and YouTube played a crucial role in connecting individuals and disseminating information during the European color revolutions. These platforms provided a space for activists to share their grievances, coordinate protests, and mobilize supporters. The ability to reach a large audience quickly and efficiently was unparalleled, allowing for the rapid spread of information and the organization of mass demonstrations.

One of the key advantages of social media was its ability to transcend physical boundaries. Activists could connect and collaborate across countries, sharing tactics and strategies that had proven successful in other revolutions. This cross-pollination of ideas and experiences contributed to the effectiveness and widespread nature of the European color revolutions.

Furthermore, social media allowed activists to challenge the dominant narratives propagated by traditional media outlets. By directly sharing their experiences and perspectives, activists were able to counteract state-controlled or biased media coverage. This gave them a platform to amplify their message and garner international attention, ultimately influencing public opinion and putting pressure on governments.

However, it is important to note that social media was not without its limitations. While it played a crucial role in mobilization and organization, it was not the sole factor behind the success of the European color revolutions. Other factors, such as economic grievances, external actors, and cultural movements, also played significant roles in shaping the outcomes of these revolutions.

In conclusion, social media played a pivotal role in the mobilization and organization of the European color revolutions. It provided a platform for activists to connect, share information, and challenge dominant narratives. However, it is essential to analyze its impact in conjunction with other factors to gain a comprehensive understanding of these historic events.

The Impact of Social Media on Protest Strategies

In recent years, social media has emerged as a powerful tool in shaping the strategies and outcomes of protests around the world. This subchapter examines the impact of social media on protest strategies during the European color revolutions, providing insights into the ways in which these movements utilized online platforms to mobilize, organize, and amplify their voices.

The European color revolutions, which occurred in various countries across the continent during the early 2000s, were marked by widespread public dissatisfaction with political regimes, corruption, and lack of democratic representation. Social media platforms such as Facebook, Twitter, and YouTube played a crucial role in these movements, providing a space for activists to connect, share information, and coordinate actions.

One key impact of social media on protest strategies was the rapid dissemination of information. Unlike traditional media, social media allowed protesters to bypass government censorship and control, enabling them to share real-time updates, images, and videos with a global audience. This increased visibility not only garnered international support but also put pressure on authorities to respond to the demands of the protesters.

Furthermore, social media facilitated the organization of protest events and the mobilization of participants. Activists could create public event pages, invite followers, and share details about the time, date, and location of demonstrations. This level of coordination was unprecedented and contributed to the mass participation seen in the European color revolutions.

Additionally, social media provided a platform for artistic expressions and cultural movements within these protests. Through platforms like Instagram and Tumblr, protesters could share artwork, poetry, and music that expressed their grievances and aspirations. This creative aspect of the movement not only helped to unify participants but also attracted the attention of a wider audience, including historians interested in exploring the cultural dimensions of these revolutions.

While social media undoubtedly played a pivotal role in the European color revolutions, it is important to acknowledge that it was not the sole determining factor. Economic factors, gender dynamics, external actors, and other variables also influenced the outcomes of these protests. Nonetheless, the impact of social media on protest strategies cannot be overlooked, as it allowed for unprecedented levels of mobilization, coordination, and visibility.

In conclusion, social media had a profound impact on the protest strategies employed during the European color revolutions. It facilitated the rapid dissemination of information, enabled the organization and mobilization of participants, and provided a space for artistic expressions and cultural movements. As historians examine the legacy and long-term effects of these revolutions on European politics, it is crucial to recognize and analyze the role of social media in shaping the dynamics and outcomes of these transformative movements.

Challenges and Limitations of Social Media in the Color Revolutions

In recent years, the role of social media in political movements has become increasingly significant, especially in the context of the European color revolutions. These revolutions, characterized by their nonviolent and peaceful nature, saw widespread use of social media platforms such as Facebook, Twitter, and YouTube as tools for organizing and mobilizing protesters. However, it is important to acknowledge the challenges and limitations that social media faced during these transformative events.

One of the key challenges of social media in the color revolutions was the digital divide. While social media platforms provided a space for activists to share information and coordinate actions, not everyone had equal access to these technologies. In many Eastern European countries, for example, the internet penetration rate was relatively low, especially among older generations. This created a divide between those who could actively participate in the online discourse and those who were left out, limiting the reach and impact of social media as a mobilization tool.

Another limitation was the issue of misinformation and propaganda. Social media platforms were not immune to the spread of fake news and disinformation campaigns. External actors and political elites often exploited these platforms to spread propaganda and manipulate public opinion. In the color revolutions, this was particularly evident in countries such as Ukraine and Georgia, where both pro-government and opposition forces used social media to shape the narrative and discredit their opponents. The challenge for historians is to navigate through this sea of information and discern the truth from the falsehoods.

Furthermore, social media's effectiveness in sustaining long-term change has been questioned. While these platforms played a vital role in mobilizing large numbers of protesters and organizing demonstrations, their impact on the actual political outcomes of the color revolutions remains debated. Some argue that social media's ability to foster collective identity and solidarity among protesters was instrumental in toppling authoritarian regimes. Others, however, contend that social media's influence was limited to the initial stages of the revolutions and did not necessarily translate into lasting political change.

In conclusion, while social media played a crucial role in the European color revolutions, it faced several challenges and limitations. The digital divide, the spread of misinformation, and the question of long-term impact all pose important considerations when analyzing the role of social media in these transformative events. By critically examining these challenges, historians can gain a deeper understanding of the complex dynamics that shaped the color revolutions and their lasting effects on European politics.

Chapter 2: Artistic Expressions and Cultural Movements in the European Color Revolutions

The Role of Street Art and Graffiti

In the context of the European color revolutions, street art and graffiti played a significant role in shaping and reflecting the movements' goals, ideologies, and expressions of dissent. This subchapter aims to explore the multifaceted role of street art and graffiti during the European color revolutions, examining their impact on the social and cultural dynamics of these transformative events.

Street art and graffiti emerged as potent forms of artistic expression that challenged the dominant narratives and power structures of the time. Artists and activists used these mediums to convey their dissatisfaction with the status quo, to demand change, and to raise awareness about the issues they deemed essential to address. By taking their messages to the streets, these artists ensured that their voices reached a broader audience, transcending traditional boundaries and engaging with people from all walks of life.

One of the significant contributions of street art and graffiti during the European color revolutions was their ability to galvanize public opinion and mobilize support for the movements. These visual displays of dissent served as powerful symbols of resistance, often becoming iconic representations of the revolutions themselves. By occupying public spaces with their art, activists created a sense of ownership and belonging among the people, fostering a collective spirit of protest and solidarity.

Moreover, street art and graffiti became crucial tools for challenging the mainstream media's narrative and propaganda during the European color revolutions. By bypassing traditional channels of communication, activists could convey alternative narratives and counter the biased coverage of the events. This subversive use of art and graffiti allowed for the dissemination of information and ideas that would have otherwise been suppressed or distorted.

Furthermore, street art and graffiti provided a platform for marginalized groups, including women, youth, and ethnic minorities, to express their grievances and demand greater inclusion in the political and social spheres. These art forms became a means of amplifying their voices, challenging gender dynamics, and promoting diversity within the movements.

Lastly, the legacy of street art and graffiti in the European color revolutions can still be seen today. These movements sparked a cultural shift, inspiring subsequent generations of artists and activists to use art as a tool for social and political change. The impact of street art and graffiti on European politics and society continues to reverberate, reminding us of the power of artistic expression in shaping our world.

In conclusion, street art and graffiti played a vital role in the European color revolutions, serving as powerful tools of resistance, mobilization, and counter-narrative. Their ability to engage and inspire a wide range of people, challenge mainstream media, and amplify marginalized voices made them crucial components of these transformative movements. The legacy of street art and graffiti endures, reminding us of the enduring power of artistic expression in shaping the course of history.

Music and Performance as Forms of Protest

Throughout history, music and performance have played pivotal roles in driving social and political change. The European color revolutions were no exception, as they witnessed the power of artistic expressions and cultural movements in mobilizing the masses and challenging established systems. This subchapter focuses on the significant role that music and performance played during these transformative periods.

Music has long been recognized as a universal language that transcends barriers and unites people. In the context of the European color revolutions, music became a powerful tool for expressing dissent and solidarity. Artists and musicians composed protest songs that captured the frustrations and aspirations of the people. These songs were not only catchy and emotionally charged, but they also conveyed powerful political messages that resonated with the masses. From the iconic anthems of the Ukrainian Euromaidan to the revolutionary melodies of the Arab Spring, music became a rallying cry for change.

Performance art also emerged as a form of protest during the European color revolutions. Theatrical plays, street performances, and flash mobs were used to convey powerful political messages and challenge the status quo. Artists utilized their creativity to create provocative and thought-provoking spectacles that captivated audiences and sparked conversations. These performances acted as catalysts for social and political dialogue, encouraging individuals to question authority and demand change.

Social media played a crucial role in amplifying the impact of music and performance as forms of protest during the European color revolutions. Platforms such as Facebook, Twitter, and YouTube allowed for the rapid dissemination of protest songs and videos, reaching a wider audience and mobilizing support. Hashtags and trending topics facilitated the organization of flash mobs and performances, enabling activists to coordinate their efforts and maximize their impact. The power of social media in spreading artistic expressions and cultural movements cannot be underestimated, as it served as a catalyst for solidarity and unity across borders.

In conclusion, music and performance emerged as potent forms of protest during the European color revolutions. Artists and musicians used their talents to create powerful protest songs that resonated with the masses, while performance art captivated audiences and sparked crucial conversations. The influence of social media further amplified the impact of these artistic expressions, fostering solidarity and mobilizing support. The European color revolutions demonstrated the enduring power of music and performance as catalysts for social and political change, leaving a lasting impact on European politics for years to come.

Literature and Poetry as Catalysts for Change

Throughout history, literature and poetry have played a significant role in shaping societies and sparking revolutions. In the context of the European color revolutions, these artistic forms of expression acted as powerful catalysts for change, mobilizing individuals and inspiring collective action. This subchapter explores the profound impact of literature and poetry on the European color revolutions, shedding light on their ability to ignite social and political transformation.

Literature, with its ability to capture the essence of societal issues, served as a mirror that reflected the grievances and aspirations of the people. It provided a platform for individuals to voice their discontent and express their desire for change. Writers and intellectuals played a crucial role in mobilizing public opinion, using their literary creations to criticize oppressive regimes and advocate for democratic reforms. Their works resonated with a wide range of individuals, transcending social, cultural, and linguistic barriers, and creating a sense of unity among diverse groups.

Similarly, poetry emerged as a powerful tool for inspiring and mobilizing people during the European color revolutions. Poets crafted verses that conveyed the hopes, dreams, and frustrations of the masses, using metaphors and vivid imagery to evoke emotions and ignite a desire for change. These poems were often recited at protests, rallies, and gatherings, serving as rallying cries that united and energized the crowds.

One notable example of the impact of literature and poetry in the European color revolutions is the role they played in galvanizing youth and student movements. Young people, often disillusioned with the existing political system, found solace and inspiration in the works of revolutionary writers and poets. These literary creations provided them with a sense of identity, purpose, and a vision for a better future. They became catalysts for youth-led movements, as young individuals organized themselves around literary circles and used literature as a tool for mobilization.

Furthermore, literature and poetry also played a crucial role in countering propaganda and shaping public opinion. In the face of state-controlled media, writers and poets provided alternative narratives that challenged the official discourse. Their works exposed the truth, debunked government propaganda, and provided an alternative perspective on the events unfolding during the European color revolutions.

In conclusion, literature and poetry acted as catalysts for change during the European color revolutions, inspiring and mobilizing individuals, shaping public opinion, and providing a voice for the marginalized. They served as powerful tools for resistance and played a significant role in the transformation of European societies. The subchapter on literature and poetry in this book aims to shed light on the profound impact of these artistic forms of expression, highlighting their role in igniting social and political change during this pivotal period in European history.

Cultural Movements and the Reclamation of National Identity

The European color revolutions were not only transformative political events but also powerful cultural movements that sparked the reclamation of national identity across the continent. These revolutions, characterized by their nonviolent nature and use of symbolism, brought about significant changes in European societies, challenging traditional power structures and inspiring citizens to embrace their cultural heritage.

One of the key aspects of the European color revolutions was the role of social media in mobilizing and organizing protests. Platforms such as Facebook and Twitter allowed activists to connect, share information, and coordinate their actions, enabling them to reach a wider audience and amplify their message. Social media became a powerful tool in shaping public opinion and challenging the narratives of the ruling regimes.

Artistic expressions and cultural movements played a crucial role in the European color revolutions, serving as a form of protest and a means of reclaiming national identity. Artists, musicians, and writers used their creative talents to express dissent, challenge the status quo, and evoke a sense of national pride. Street art, music festivals, and literary works became powerful mediums through which people could connect with their cultural heritage and express their aspirations for change.

The impact of economic factors on the European color revolutions cannot be overlooked. High unemployment rates, economic inequality, and corruption were common grievances that fueled the protests. Citizens demanded fairer economic systems and opportunities for all, in addition to political reforms. Economic factors often intersected with cultural and national identity issues, highlighting the complex and interconnected nature of the revolutions.

Gender dynamics and feminism also played a significant role in the European color revolutions. Women activists and feminist movements contributed to the protests, demanding equal rights, reproductive rights, and an end to gender-based violence and discrimination. The revolutions provided a platform for women to challenge patriarchal norms and advocate for gender equality, leaving a lasting impact on European societies.

External actors, such as international organizations, neighboring countries, and global media, influenced the European color revolutions. Support from these actors, whether through funding, diplomatic pressure, or media coverage, had an impact on the outcomes and the perception of the revolutions. The involvement of external actors raised questions about sovereignty and the balance of power in European politics.

In conclusion, the cultural movements and the reclamation of national identity were integral parts of the European color revolutions. Social media, artistic expressions, economic factors, gender dynamics, external actors, and other elements interacted to shape these transformative events. Understanding the cultural dimensions of the revolutions is essential to fully grasp their lasting effects on European politics and society.

Chapter 3: The Impact of Economic Factors on the European Color Revolutions

Economic Inequality as a Catalyst for Protest

In the subchapter "Economic Inequality as a Catalyst for Protest" of the book "A Tapestry of Change: Comparative Analysis of the European Color Revolutions," we delve into the profound impact of economic factors on the European color revolutions. This section aims to provide historians and scholars with a comprehensive understanding of how economic inequality played a pivotal role in sparking and fueling these transformative movements.

Throughout Europe, societal discontent and frustration with economic inequality reached a boiling point during the color revolutions. The glaring wealth disparities, coupled with stagnant wages and rising living costs, created a breeding ground for widespread social unrest. This chapter explores the ways in which economic grievances acted as a catalyst for the protests, driving individuals from various socio-economic backgrounds to take to the streets.

By analyzing the differing economic landscapes of countries such as Ukraine, Georgia, and Serbia, we can identify commonalities and divergences in how economic factors influenced the revolutions. Factors such as corruption, crony capitalism, and lack of economic opportunities were central to the grievances expressed by protestors. The subchapter provides an in-depth analysis of the economic systems and policies in these countries, highlighting the specific injustices that mobilized the population.

Furthermore, this section explores the role of social media in amplifying economic grievances and facilitating organization and mobilization during the color revolutions. The advent of digital platforms provided a powerful tool for activists to spread their message, unite disparate groups, and expose the economic disparities that fueled their discontent. We examine the ways in which social media platforms acted as a catalyst for protest, giving marginalized voices a global stage and facilitating the coordination of mass demonstrations.

By delving into the economic factors that underpinned the European color revolutions, this subchapter sheds light on the complex relationship between wealth disparities and social change. It provides historians with a nuanced understanding of the socio-economic dynamics that propelled these movements and offers valuable insights into the broader implications for European politics and society.

As we navigate the contemporary world, where economic inequality remains a pressing issue, the lessons learned from the European color revolutions are more relevant than ever. By examining the role of economic factors in these revolutions, historians can gain valuable insights into the potential for future social movements and the long-term effects of addressing economic inequality on European politics and society.

Corruption and the Fight for Transparency

In the tumultuous landscape of the European color revolutions, corruption emerged as a critical issue that fueled discontent and sparked widespread protests. This subchapter delves into the intricate relationship between corruption and the fight for transparency, shedding light on the pivotal role it played in the revolutionary movements across Europe.

As historians, it is essential to understand that corruption was not merely a symptom of the prevailing political and economic systems; it was a catalyst for change. The subversive power of corruption was magnified by the emergence of social media, which acted as a powerful tool for mobilization and information dissemination. Citizens, armed with smartphones and social networking platforms, broadcasted instances of corruption, bringing them to the forefront of public consciousness.

Artistic expressions and cultural movements also played a crucial role in exposing corruption and fueling the fight for transparency. The European color revolutions witnessed an explosion of creativity, with artists and cultural movements using their voices to challenge the corrupt status quo. Street art, music, and theater became powerful vehicles for dissent, uniting diverse groups and igniting a collective desire for change.

At the heart of corruption lay economic factors that perpetuated inequality and disenfranchisement. The subchapter explores the impact of economic disparities on the European color revolutions, highlighting how economic grievances and the desire for a fairer distribution of wealth fueled the protests. The corruption within financial institutions and the close ties between political elites and business magnates were exposed, further fueling public anger.

Gender dynamics and feminism within the European color revolutions also deserve attention. The subchapter analyzes how women played a crucial role in the fight against corruption, as they confronted not only political and economic injustices but also deep-rooted gender inequalities. Feminist movements emerged, demanding not only transparency but also gender equality and the recognition of women's rights within the revolutionary discourse.

Furthermore, the influence of external actors on the European color revolutions cannot be overlooked. The subchapter explores how foreign governments, international organizations, and non-governmental organizations either supported or obstructed the fight against corruption, shaping the trajectory of the revolutions.

By analyzing corruption and the fight for transparency in a comparative manner across different countries, historians can unravel the unique dynamics and lessons learned from each revolution. The subchapter provides a comprehensive overview of the European color revolutions, highlighting commonalities and differences, ultimately contributing to a deeper understanding of this transformative period in European history.

Lastly, it delves into the legacy and long-term effects of the European color revolutions on European politics. Did the revolutions succeed in establishing transparent and accountable systems? Or did corruption find new ways to persist? By examining the lasting impact, historians can draw valuable insights into the endurance of corrupt practices and the ongoing struggle for transparency in European politics.

In conclusion, corruption was a central theme in the European color revolutions, sparking protests and driving demands for transparency. The subchapter explores the multifaceted nature of corruption, addressing its relationship with social media, artistic expressions, economic factors, gender dynamics, external actors, and long-term consequences. By dissecting corruption and the fight for transparency, historians can contribute to a nuanced understanding of this transformative period in European history.

Labor Movements and Worker Unrest

The European color revolutions of the early 21st century were not solely driven by political dissent and demands for democratic reforms. They were also deeply influenced by labor movements and worker unrest, which played a significant role in shaping the outcomes of these revolutions. This subchapter explores the intricate relationship between labor movements, worker unrest, and the European color revolutions.

Labor movements have long been a key driving force behind social and political change, and their impact on the European color revolutions was no exception. Workers across various industries, including manufacturing, transportation, and services, organized strikes, protests, and demonstrations to voice their grievances and demand better working conditions, fair wages, and the protection of workers' rights.

The role of social media in the European color revolutions cannot be understated. Platforms like Facebook, Twitter, and YouTube provided a powerful means for workers to mobilize, share information, and coordinate their actions. Through social media, workers were able to reach a wider audience, garner support, and amplify their message, ultimately contributing to the success of the revolutions.

Artistic expressions and cultural movements also played a significant role in the European color revolutions. Artists, musicians, and writers used their creative talents to raise awareness about the struggles of workers and the injustices they faced. Their works served as a catalyst for public discourse and helped galvanize support for the labor movements, inspiring people from all walks of life to join the cause.

Economic factors were another important driver of worker unrest during the European color revolutions. The impact of economic crises, austerity measures, and widening income inequality fueled the discontent of workers, pushing them to take to the streets and demand change. The revolutions themselves also had profound economic implications, leading to reforms in labor laws, the establishment of fairer trade practices, and the redistribution of wealth.

Gender dynamics and feminism were inherent within the European color revolutions, as women workers played a vital role in driving change. Female workers faced unique challenges and discrimination in the workplace, and their participation in labor movements and worker unrest was crucial in challenging gender disparities and advocating for gender equality.

External actors, such as international labor organizations, also played a significant role in supporting and influencing the European color revolutions. These organizations provided resources, expertise, and solidarity to the labor movements, further amplifying their demands and contributing to their success.

In conclusion, the labor movements and worker unrest during the European color revolutions were integral to shaping the trajectory and outcomes of these historic events. The mobilization of workers, the use of social media, artistic expressions, economic factors, gender dynamics, and the influence of external actors all worked together to create a powerful force for change. The legacy and long-term effects of these labor movements can still be seen in the transformed political landscape of Europe today.

The Role of Economic Sanctions and International Pressure

Title: The Role of Economic Sanctions and International Pressure

Introduction:

In the tumultuous landscape of the European color revolutions, the role of economic sanctions and international pressure cannot be overlooked. This subchapter delves into the intricate web of economic factors and external actors that influenced and shaped the course of these historic events. By examining the impact of economic sanctions and international pressure, we can gain a comprehensive understanding of the complex dynamics that unfolded during these transformative periods.

Economic Sanctions: Catalysts for Change

Economic sanctions played a pivotal role in the European color revolutions, acting as catalysts for change. These measures, imposed by external actors, aimed to pressure autocratic regimes by restricting trade, freezing assets, and limiting access to international markets. By crippling the economic foundations of oppressive regimes, sanctions created severe societal and political consequences, ultimately fueling the revolutionary fervor among the masses.

International Pressure: A Global Call for Democracy

Simultaneously, the European color revolutions witnessed immense international pressure exerted by democratic nations and supranational organizations. These actors, driven by a commitment to democratic values and human rights, used diplomatic channels, public condemnations, and grassroots movements to advocate for political change. Their collective voice not only served as a moral compass but also provided invaluable support to the revolutionaries on the ground, emboldening their struggle for freedom and democracy.

The Economic Factor: A Driving Force

Beyond sanctions and international pressure, economic factors played a crucial role in shaping the European color revolutions. Rising inequality, corruption, and economic stagnation emerged as key grievances driving public discontent. The revolutions saw vibrant youth and student movements demanding economic reforms, job opportunities, and social justice. As economic factors intersected with political demands, the revolutions took on a multidimensional character, challenging not only autocratic rule but also the prevailing economic order.

Conclusion:

The role of economic sanctions and international pressure in the European color revolutions cannot be overstated. These powerful forces interacted with a range of factors, from social media and artistic expressions to gender dynamics and environmental activism, shaping the trajectory and outcomes of these transformative events. As historians, understanding the interplay between economic factors, external actors, and revolutionary movements is essential to comprehending the legacy and long-term effects of the European color revolutions on European politics. By exploring this multifaceted tapestry of change, we can unlock invaluable insights into the complex nature of social and political transformation.

Chapter 4: Gender Dynamics and Feminism within the European Color Revolutions

Women's Leadership and Participation in Protests

In the backdrop of the European color revolutions, one aspect that has emerged as a significant force is the active involvement and leadership of women in these protests. This subchapter aims to explore the role of women in the European color revolutions, highlighting their contributions, challenges, and the impact they have had on the overall outcome of these movements.

Throughout history, women have played crucial roles in social and political movements, and the European color revolutions are no exception. Women have not only participated in large numbers in these protests but have also assumed leadership positions, challenging traditional gender roles and societal expectations. Their involvement has been instrumental in shaping the course of these revolutions and bringing about meaningful change.

One of the key factors that have enabled women's participation in these protests is the rise of social media. Platforms like Facebook, Twitter, and Instagram have provided women with a powerful tool to mobilize and organize themselves, allowing them to transcend geographical boundaries and connect with like-minded individuals. Through social media, women have been able to share their experiences, voice their demands, and strategize effectively, thus amplifying their influence within the movements.

Furthermore, the European color revolutions have witnessed the emergence of artistic expressions and cultural movements that have been instrumental in galvanizing support and mobilizing the masses. Women have actively participated in these artistic and cultural endeavors, using their creativity and expression to convey powerful messages of resistance and change. Their artistic contributions have not only added depth and vibrancy to the protests but have also served as a means to challenge societal norms and advocate for gender equality.

However, it is important to acknowledge that women's participation in the European color revolutions has not been without challenges. Women have often faced discrimination, harassment, and violence, both within the protests and from external actors. Despite these obstacles, women have persevered, demonstrating resilience and determination in their quest for justice and equality.

The impact of women's leadership and participation in the European color revolutions cannot be understated. Their involvement has challenged traditional power structures, brought attention to gender dynamics and feminism, and paved the way for greater gender equality within the broader political landscape. The influence and contributions of women in these protests have left a lasting legacy on European politics, inspiring future generations and shaping the trajectory of social and political movements.

In conclusion, women's leadership and participation in the European color revolutions have been pivotal in driving meaningful change. Their active involvement, supported by social media platforms and artistic expressions, has challenged societal norms and brought attention to gender dynamics within these movements. The impact of their contributions will continue to shape European politics and inspire future generations to strive for a more inclusive and equal society.

Feminist Movements and Demands for Gender Equality

The European color revolutions of the 21st century brought about significant social and political changes across the continent. While much of the focus has been on the role of social media, artistic expressions, economic factors, and external actors, it is essential not to overlook the crucial role played by feminist movements and their demands for gender equality.

Throughout history, women have been at the forefront of social and political movements fighting for their rights. The European color revolutions were no exception, as women actively participated and demanded equal treatment and opportunities. These movements were driven by a desire to challenge patriarchal structures and address the systemic discrimination faced by women in various spheres of life.

One of the key demands put forth by feminist movements during the European color revolutions was equal political representation. Women demanded a seat at the decision-making table, advocating for gender parity in government bodies and institutions. They argued that their perspectives and experiences were essential for creating inclusive and representative policies.

Additionally, feminist movements called for an end to gender-based violence and the implementation of laws and policies that protect women's rights. They highlighted the prevalence of domestic violence, sexual assault, and harassment, and demanded justice for the victims. Through protests, awareness campaigns, and advocacy, these movements brought attention to the urgent need for societal change.

Furthermore, feminist movements within the European color revolutions sought to challenge traditional gender roles and stereotypes. They aimed to break down the barriers that limited women's access to education, employment, and economic opportunities. By advocating for equal pay and equal career advancement prospects, they fought to dismantle the gendered division of labor that perpetuated inequalities.

The impact of feminist movements and their demands for gender equality cannot be underestimated. They played a crucial role in shaping the narrative of the European color revolutions and contributed to the broader goal of creating a more inclusive and equitable society. Their efforts paved the way for legislative reforms, increased awareness, and a shift in societal attitudes towards gender equality.

As historians, it is essential to recognize and study the contributions of feminist movements within the European color revolutions. By understanding their goals, strategies, and achievements, we can gain valuable insights into the dynamics of social and political change and the ongoing struggle for gender equality in Europe.

Addressing Patriarchy and Gender-Based Violence

In the subchapter "Addressing Patriarchy and Gender-Based Violence," we delve into an often overlooked aspect of the European color revolutions: the gender dynamics and feminism within these transformative movements. While the revolutions were primarily driven by demands for democracy, freedom, and social justice, it is important to examine how they intersected with the fight against patriarchal structures and gender-based violence.

Throughout history, patriarchal norms and gender inequality have been deeply entrenched in European societies. However, the European color revolutions provided a platform for individuals and groups to challenge these oppressive structures and advocate for gender equality. Women played a significant role in these movements, both as leaders and as active participants, demanding their rights and challenging the prevailing norms.

One significant aspect that emerged during the color revolutions was the prevalence of gender-based violence. Activists and scholars alike recognized the need to address this issue head-on, as it hindered progress and threatened the safety and well-being of women participating in the revolutions. This subchapter explores the strategies employed to combat gender-based violence, such as the establishment of safe spaces, the creation of support networks, and the implementation of policies to punish perpetrators.

Furthermore, this subchapter delves into the feminist movements that emerged during and after the color revolutions. These movements sought to challenge not only the overt manifestations of patriarchy but also the subtle and systemic forms of gender inequality. Activists utilized social media platforms to raise awareness, organize protests, and share stories, fostering a sense of solidarity among women across different countries.

The subchapter also highlights the role of external actors, such as international organizations and NGOs, in supporting feminist movements within the color revolutions. These actors played a crucial role in providing resources, advocating for gender equality, and pressuring governments to address gender-based violence.

Ultimately, the efforts to address patriarchy and gender-based violence within the European color revolutions had a lasting impact on European politics. They helped pave the way for greater gender equality, representation, and participation in subsequent political processes. By examining this crucial aspect of the color revolutions, historians can gain a deeper understanding of the multifaceted nature of these transformative movements and their long-term effects on European societies.

Intersectionality and the Inclusion of Marginalized Voices

In the midst of the European color revolutions, a crucial aspect that often goes unnoticed is the role of intersectionality and the inclusion of marginalized voices. These revolutions, which swept across various European countries, were marked by a desire for political and social change. However, it is vital to acknowledge that these movements were not homogenous, but rather comprised of individuals from diverse backgrounds, each with their own unique struggles and grievances.

The concept of intersectionality, coined by legal scholar Kimberlé Crenshaw, recognizes that individuals can experience multiple forms of oppression simultaneously, which can further marginalize their voices. In the context of the European color revolutions, intersectionality played a significant role in shaping the dynamics of the movements and the demands put forth by the protestors.

One of the key aspects of intersectionality within the European color revolutions was the inclusion of marginalized groups such as ethnic minorities, LGBTQ+ individuals, and disabled communities. These groups, who often face discrimination and exclusion in their daily lives, found a platform within the revolution to voice their concerns and demand equal rights and opportunities. Their involvement not only added strength and diversity to the movements but also highlighted the intersection of various forms of oppression.

Furthermore, intersectionality also intersected with other niches within the European color revolutions. For example, the role of social media in amplifying marginalized voices cannot be underestimated. Platforms like Facebook, Twitter, and YouTube allowed individuals from marginalized communities to share their stories, mobilize support, and challenge the dominant narratives propagated by traditional media outlets. This marked a significant shift in the way information was disseminated during these revolutions.

Artistic expressions and cultural movements also played a crucial role in giving visibility to marginalized voices. Through art, music, and performance, individuals were able to express their grievances and demand change. These artistic expressions not only fostered solidarity among different marginalized groups but also served as a powerful tool for raising awareness among the wider public.

It is important to note that the inclusion of marginalized voices was not without challenges. Intersectionality brought to the forefront tensions and conflicts within the movements, as different groups had differing priorities and demands. However, the recognition of these tensions and the willingness to engage in dialogue and collaboration allowed for a more inclusive and representative movement.

Ultimately, the inclusion of marginalized voices within the European color revolutions was a crucial step towards achieving a more equitable and just society. By acknowledging the intersecting forms of oppression faced by individuals, these movements were able to challenge the status quo and demand meaningful change. This subchapter seeks to shed light on the significance of intersectionality and the inclusion of marginalized voices within the broader context of the European color revolutions, highlighting their contributions and the challenges faced along the way.

Chapter 5: The Influence of External Actors on the European Color Revolutions

Russia's Role in the Color Revolutions

The European Color Revolutions, a series of popular uprisings that swept across various countries in the early 2000s, were marked by their use of social media, artistic expressions, and economic factors. These revolutions also witnessed the involvement of external actors, including Russia, which played a significant role in shaping their outcomes. This subchapter delves into Russia's role in the Color Revolutions, shedding light on its influence and impact.

Russia's involvement in the Color Revolutions was multifaceted, encompassing both direct and indirect means. From a historical perspective, Russia viewed these revolutions as a threat to its sphere of influence, particularly in neighboring countries such as Ukraine, Georgia, and Moldova. As such, it sought to counter these movements by employing various strategies, including economic pressure, propaganda, and support for pro-Russian political factions.

One crucial aspect of Russia's involvement was its exploitation of social media platforms. Recognizing the power of these platforms in mobilizing and organizing protests, Russia employed a range of tactics to manipulate online narratives and spread disinformation. This included the creation of fake social media accounts, the dissemination of misleading information, and the amplification of pro-Russian voices. By doing so, Russia aimed to undermine the credibility of the Color Revolutions and maintain its influence in the region.

Additionally, Russia utilized its economic leverage to exert pressure on countries undergoing these revolutions. By leveraging its control over energy resources, Russia could impose economic sanctions or offer financial incentives to sway political outcomes. This economic influence played a critical role in shaping the trajectory of these revolutions, as countries had to weigh their desire for change against the potential consequences of angering Russia.

Furthermore, Russia also supported pro-Russian political factions and used its state-controlled media to disseminate propaganda. This propaganda aimed to discredit the goals of the Color Revolutions, portraying them as Western-backed movements seeking to undermine Russian interests. By framing the revolutions in this manner, Russia sought to delegitimize their demands and maintain its influence in the region.

Russia's role in the Color Revolutions extended beyond its direct involvement. The outcomes of these revolutions had a lasting impact on European politics, leading to shifts in power dynamics and the emergence of new political actors. Russia's influence during this period helped shape the legacy and long-term effects of the Color Revolutions, as their outcomes had a significant impact on Russia's relations with European countries.

In conclusion, Russia played a crucial role in the European Color Revolutions through its manipulation of social media, economic pressure, and support for pro-Russian political factions. Its involvement was driven by a desire to maintain its influence in the region and counter what it perceived as a threat to its sphere of influence. Understanding Russia's role in the Color Revolutions is essential for historians analyzing the broader context and impact of these revolutionary movements.

The European Union's Response and Influence

The European Union (EU) played a significant role in responding to and influencing the European color revolutions. These revolutions, which took place across various countries in Europe, were characterized by mass protests, demands for political change, and the use of social media as a catalyst for mobilization. Historians studying these events must consider the EU's response and influence as an important factor in understanding their outcomes.

One of the key ways in which the EU responded to the color revolutions was through diplomatic channels. The EU actively engaged with the governments and opposition groups involved, seeking to mediate and facilitate dialogue. By doing so, the EU aimed to promote peaceful resolutions and democratic reforms. This diplomatic involvement helped shape the trajectory of the revolutions and influenced the subsequent political developments in these countries.

Furthermore, the EU's response to the color revolutions was also reflected in its policies and financial support. The EU provided financial assistance to countries undergoing political transitions, helping to stabilize their economies and support democratic reforms. This support was crucial in ensuring the success of these revolutions and their long-term impact on European politics.

In addition to its response, the EU also exerted influence on the European color revolutions. The EU's promotion of democratic values and norms through its enlargement process and conditionality requirements had a profound impact on the countries involved. The prospect of EU membership served as a powerful incentive for these countries to undertake democratic reforms and address issues of corruption and human rights abuses. As such, the EU's influence played a significant role in shaping the direction and outcomes of the color revolutions.

Moreover, the EU's response and influence were not limited to politics and diplomacy. The EU also played a role in supporting and fostering cultural movements and artistic expressions during the color revolutions.

Through cultural exchange programs and funding initiatives, the EU empowered artists and activists to voice their aspirations for political change. This artistic dimension of the color revolutions contributed to their overall impact and legacy as transformative social movements.

In conclusion, the European Union's response and influence were crucial in shaping the European color revolutions. Through diplomatic engagement, financial support, and the promotion of democratic values, the EU played a significant role in facilitating peaceful resolutions and pushing for democratic reforms. Its influence extended beyond politics to encompass cultural movements and artistic expressions. Historians studying the European color revolutions must take into account the EU's response and influence as key factors in understanding the dynamics and outcomes of these historic events.

US Involvement and Promotion of Democracy

The European color revolutions were a series of political movements that swept across several countries in Europe during the late 20th and early 21st centuries. These revolutions were characterized by their use of peaceful protests, vibrant imagery, and a desire for democratic change. While the origins and outcomes of these revolutions varied from country to country, one common thread throughout many of them was the involvement and promotion of democracy by the United States.

The United States played a significant role in the European color revolutions, providing support and encouragement to those seeking democratic change. This support was often manifested through various means, such as financial aid, training programs for activists, and diplomatic pressure on authoritarian regimes. The US government saw these revolutions as an opportunity to promote its own democratic ideals and advance its geopolitical interests in the region.

One key aspect of US involvement in the European color revolutions was the role of social media. The rise of platforms like Facebook and Twitter provided a new and powerful tool for organizing and mobilizing protesters. Activists used these platforms to spread their message, coordinate actions, and connect with like-minded individuals across borders. The US government recognized the potential of social media in promoting democracy and actively supported initiatives that aimed to increase internet access and digital literacy in these countries.

Another important dimension of US involvement was the support for artistic expressions and cultural movements within the European color revolutions. Artistic expressions, such as murals, graffiti, and music, played a crucial role in shaping the visual identity of these movements and capturing the attention of the public. The US government funded cultural exchange programs, art installations, and festivals that promoted freedom of expression and encouraged artistic activism.

Additionally, the US recognized the importance of economic factors in fueling the desire for democratic change. Economic grievances, such as high unemployment rates and income inequality, often served as catalysts for these revolutions. The US government provided economic assistance and encouraged foreign direct investment in these countries to alleviate these issues and promote stability.

While the US involvement in the European color revolutions was driven by a desire to promote democracy, it was not without controversy. Critics argued that US support for these movements was driven by self-interest and a desire to influence the geopolitical landscape in Europe. They pointed to instances where US support was provided to groups that had questionable democratic credentials or had connections to extremist ideologies.

Overall, the US played a significant role in the European color revolutions by providing support and promotion of democratic ideals.

Whether through social media, artistic expressions, economic assistance, or diplomatic pressure, the US government sought to empower those seeking democratic change and shape the course of these revolutions. The long-term effects of US involvement in these revolutions continue to be debated and analyzed by historians, as they have had a lasting impact on European politics and the broader global landscape.

China's Reaction to the European Color Revolutions

The European color revolutions of the early 2000s, including the Orange Revolution in Ukraine, the Rose Revolution in Georgia, and the Tulip Revolution in Kyrgyzstan, were important milestones in the history of democratic movements. These revolutions, characterized by their use of social media, artistic expressions, and youth activism, had significant impacts on European politics and societies. However, the influence of these movements extended beyond Europe, catching the attention of external actors such as China.

China, a country known for its unique political system and restrictive approach to civil liberties, closely watched the developments of the European color revolutions. The Chinese government, led by the Communist Party, had concerns about the potential influence and implications of these movements on their own domestic stability. China's reaction to the European color revolutions can be analyzed through various lenses, including their response to social media, their engagement with external actors, and their perception of the long-term effects of these revolutions.

One significant aspect of China's reaction to the European color revolutions was their response to the role of social media. The revolutions utilized platforms like Facebook and Twitter to mobilize supporters, spread information, and challenge established narratives. China, however, has a strict internet censorship regime known as the Great Firewall, which limits access to foreign social media platforms and regulates online content. In response to the European color revolutions, China further strengthened its internet controls, implementing stricter regulations and surveillance measures to prevent the spread of dissent and maintain social stability.

Another dimension of China's reaction was its engagement with external actors involved in the European color revolutions. China, being a major global power, sought to protect its interests and influence in the regions where these revolutions took place. The Chinese government closely monitored the involvement of Western countries and organizations, perceiving them as potential threats to its own political system. China strategically used its economic leverage and diplomatic channels to counterbalance the influence of external actors and prevent similar movements from emerging within its own borders.

Furthermore, China assessed the long-term effects of the European color revolutions on European politics and societies. While the revolutions brought about significant changes in some countries, China viewed them with skepticism, emphasizing the instability and chaos that often followed these movements. The Chinese government believed that its own political system, based on authoritarian governance and economic development, provided a more stable and prosperous alternative to the democratic experiments in Europe.

In conclusion, China's reaction to the European color revolutions was shaped by its concerns about the potential spillover effects and challenges to its own political stability. China responded to these revolutions by strengthening its internet controls, engaging with external actors strategically, and questioning the long-term effects of democratic movements. Understanding China's perspective on the European color revolutions provides valuable insights into the dynamics of global politics and the contrasting approaches to governance and civil liberties.

Chapter 6: Comparative Analysis of the European Color Revolutions in Different Countries

Ukraine: The Orange Revolution

The Orange Revolution, which took place in Ukraine from late 2004 to early 2005, was a pivotal moment in the country's history and had significant implications for European politics. This subchapter will delve into the various aspects of the Orange Revolution, analyzing its causes, impact, and long-term effects.

One crucial aspect to consider is the role of social media in the European color revolutions, including the Orange Revolution. The advent of platforms like Facebook and Twitter allowed for unprecedented mobilization and coordination among protesters, making it easier to disseminate information, organize rallies, and challenge government narratives.

Furthermore, artistic expressions and cultural movements played a significant role in the Orange Revolution. Artists, musicians, and writers used their creative talents to convey the ideals and aspirations of the protesters, giving voice to their demands for democracy and political change.

Economic factors also played a crucial role in the Orange Revolution. The dissatisfaction with corruption and economic inequality fueled the protests, as Ukrainians demanded a fairer distribution of wealth and opportunities. This subchapter will explore the impact of these economic factors on the revolution and its aftermath.

Another important aspect to examine is the gender dynamics and feminism within the European color revolutions, including the Orange

Revolution. Women played a prominent role in the protests, challenging traditional gender roles and advocating for gender equality. This subchapter will delve into the feminist movements that emerged during the revolution and their long-term effects on Ukrainian society.

External actors also had a significant influence on the Orange Revolution. This subchapter will analyze the involvement of international organizations, such as the European Union and NATO, as well as neighboring countries like Russia, in shaping the outcome of the revolution.

Comparative analysis of the European color revolutions in different countries will also be explored, allowing historians to understand the similarities and differences between these movements and their respective contexts.

The role of youth and student movements in the Orange Revolution will be examined, highlighting the energy and idealism brought by younger generations to the protests and their impact on the political landscape.

Moreover, this subchapter will address the environmental activism and sustainability aspects of the Orange Revolution, shedding light on the importance of ecological concerns and the role they played in mobilizing protesters.

Media coverage and propaganda during the Orange Revolution will also be discussed, analyzing how different narratives and images shaped public opinion and influenced the outcome of the protests.

Finally, the legacy and long-term effects of the Orange Revolution on European politics will be examined. This subchapter will assess the impact of the revolution on Ukraine's political system, as well as its implications for other European countries experiencing similar challenges.

In conclusion, this subchapter on the Orange Revolution offers a comprehensive analysis of the various aspects that shaped this pivotal moment in Ukrainian and European history. By exploring the role of social media, artistic expressions, economic factors, gender dynamics, external actors, youth movements, environmental activism, media coverage, and the long-term effects, historians can gain a thorough understanding of the profound impact the Orange Revolution had on European politics.

Georgia: The Rose Revolution

The Rose Revolution is one of the most prominent events in the history of Georgia, marking a turning point in the country's political landscape. This subchapter explores the details of this revolution, focusing on its causes, key actors, and the lasting impact it had on Georgian politics.

The Rose Revolution in Georgia took place in 2003 and was a nonviolent movement that led to the overthrow of President Eduard Shevardnadze's government. It was named after the symbol of a rose, which represented the peaceful nature of the revolution. The revolution was driven by a combination of social, economic, and political factors, which had been building up over time.

Social media played a crucial role in the Rose Revolution, allowing activists to mobilize and organize protests. Platforms like Facebook, Twitter, and blogging sites provided a space for people to share information, coordinate actions, and voice their frustrations with the government. This subchapter delves into the ways social media empowered the Georgian people and facilitated their fight for political change.

Artistic expressions and cultural movements also played a significant role in the Rose Revolution. Artists, musicians, and writers used their creative talents to inspire and unite the Georgian population. This subchapter explores the various forms of artistic expressions during the revolution and how they contributed to the overall atmosphere of change.

Economic factors were another key aspect of the Rose Revolution. Widespread corruption, economic mismanagement, and poverty were major grievances of the Georgian people. This subchapter analyzes how economic factors influenced the revolution and the subsequent changes in Georgia's economic policies.

Gender dynamics and feminism within the Rose Revolution is another important aspect to explore. Women played a significant role in the revolution, challenging traditional gender norms and advocating for women's rights. This subchapter delves into the experiences of women during the revolution and the impact it had on gender dynamics in Georgian society.

External actors also influenced the Rose Revolution. This subchapter examines the role of international organizations, such as the European Union and the United States, in supporting the Georgian opposition and shaping the outcome of the revolution.

Furthermore, this subchapter offers a comparative analysis of the Rose Revolution with other European color revolutions, such as the Orange Revolution in Ukraine and the Velvet Revolution in Czechoslovakia. It highlights the similarities and differences between these revolutions and their long-term effects on European politics.

Overall, this subchapter sheds light on the Rose Revolution in Georgia, providing historians with a comprehensive understanding of its causes, key actors, and the enduring impact it had on Georgian politics. By examining the role of social media, artistic expressions, economic factors, gender dynamics, external actors, and providing a comparative analysis, this subchapter contributes to the larger narrative of the European color revolutions and their legacy on European politics.

Serbia: The Bulldozer Revolution

The Bulldozer Revolution in Serbia marked a significant turning point in the history of the European color revolutions. The revolution, which took place in 2000, saw the ousting of Slobodan Milošević, who had been in power for over a decade. This subchapter aims to provide insight into the key aspects and implications of this revolution, particularly in relation to the broader themes explored in the book.

One aspect that distinguished the Bulldozer Revolution was the role of social media. It was one of the first color revolutions where social media platforms, such as email, online forums, and text messaging, played a crucial role in organizing protests and disseminating information. The use of technology allowed for coordination and mobilization on an unprecedented scale, effectively challenging the oppressive regime.

Artistic expressions and cultural movements also played a vital role in the Bulldozer Revolution. Artists and intellectuals used their creativity and influence to raise awareness about political corruption and human rights violations. Through street performances, graffiti, and other forms of artistic expression, they were able to engage and mobilize the public, creating a sense of unity and resistance.

Economic factors were significant in Serbia's revolution. The country was grappling with a deteriorating economy, rampant corruption, and high unemployment rates. These economic hardships fueled grievances and discontent among the population, leading to widespread protests and demands for change.

Gender dynamics and feminism within the revolution were also noteworthy. Women played a prominent role in organizing and participating in protests, challenging traditional gender roles and advocating for gender equality. The revolution provided a platform for feminist activism, and its impact was felt long after its conclusion.

External actors also influenced the Bulldozer Revolution. International organizations, such as the European Union and NATO, provided support and legitimacy to the opposition movement. Their involvement highlighted the significance of external actors in shaping the outcomes of color revolutions.

The Bulldozer Revolution's legacy and long-term effects on European politics were profound. It demonstrated the power of people's movements to bring about political change and inspired other color revolutions across Europe. The revolution also led to a reevaluation of democracy and governance in Serbia, paving the way for future developments in the country.

In conclusion, the Bulldozer Revolution in Serbia exemplified the key themes explored in this book, such as the role of social media, artistic expressions, economic factors, gender dynamics, external actors, and the long-term impact of color revolutions. Its significance in the European context cannot be overstated, and its lessons continue to shape the political landscape of the continent.

Moldova: The Grape Revolution

Moldova, a small landlocked country in Eastern Europe, may not be the first place that comes to mind when discussing the European color revolutions. However, Moldova played a significant role in this transformative wave of political and social change. Known as the Grape Revolution, this subchapter explores the unique dynamics and factors that shaped Moldova's path towards democracy and its lasting impact on European politics.

The Grape Revolution, which took place in 2009, was marked by widespread protests and political upheaval. The catalyst for this revolution was the parliamentary elections, which were marred by accusations of voter fraud and corruption. Moldova's disillusioned and frustrated citizens took to the streets, demanding transparency, accountability, and change.

One crucial aspect of the Grape Revolution was the role of social media. Moldova's youth, fueled by their desire for change, utilized various online platforms to organize protests, share information, and mobilize their peers. This subchapter delves into the ways in which social media empowered the Moldovan people and facilitated their collective action.

Additionally, the Grape Revolution witnessed the emergence of artistic expressions and cultural movements. Moldovan artists, writers, musicians, and filmmakers used their creative talents to capture the spirit of the revolution and amplify its message. This subchapter explores the various artistic forms that emerged during this period and their impact on the broader movement.

Economic factors also played a significant role in the Grape Revolution. Moldova, one of Europe's poorest countries, struggled with high unemployment rates and widespread poverty. This subchapter examines how economic grievances and aspirations for a better future fueled the protests and contributed to the demands for change.

Furthermore, this subchapter delves into the gender dynamics and feminism within the Grape Revolution. Moldova, like many post-Soviet countries, faced gender disparities and discrimination. The revolution provided a platform for women's voices to be heard and their rights to be recognized. It analyzes the unique challenges faced by women in the revolution and the long-term impact on gender equality in Moldova.

The influence of external actors on the Grape Revolution is another crucial aspect explored in this subchapter. Moldova's geopolitical location made it susceptible to external influences, particularly from Russia and the European Union. It examines the role of these external actors and their impact on the revolution's outcome.

In conclusion, the subchapter "Moldova: The Grape Revolution" sheds light on the unique dynamics that shaped Moldova's path towards democracy and the profound impact it had on European politics. From the role of social media to artistic expressions, economic factors, gender dynamics, external influences, and more, this subchapter offers a comprehensive analysis of the Grape Revolution and its lasting legacy. Historians and those interested in the European color revolutions will gain valuable insights into the intricate web of factors that contributed to this transformative period in Moldova's history.

Chapter 7: The Role of Youth and Student Movements in the European Color Revolutions

Student Activism and Demand for Political Change

Student activism played a significant role in the European color revolutions, fueling the demand for political change and inspiring mass movements across the continent. This subchapter explores the impact and influence of student movements on these historic events.

During the European color revolutions, students emerged as key actors in demanding political change and challenging the status quo. Their role was crucial in mobilizing the masses, utilizing social media platforms to organize protests, disseminate information, and coordinate actions. The power of social media became evident as it facilitated rapid communication and mobilization, allowing student movements to transcend national borders and unite with like-minded individuals across Europe.

Artistic expressions and cultural movements also played a significant role in the European color revolutions. Students utilized art, music, and theater as powerful tools to express their discontent, challenge authorities, and inspire collective action. Creative forms of protest, such as street performances and graffiti, became iconic symbols of resistance and solidarity.

The demand for political change during the European color revolutions was not solely driven by ideological motives. Economic factors also played a crucial role in fueling discontent among students. High unemployment rates, economic inequality, and corruption fueled the frustration and inspired students to demand a fairer and more just society.

Gender dynamics and feminism were also prominent within the European color revolutions. Women played a vital role in student activism, challenging traditional gender roles and advocating for gender equality. Feminist movements within the color revolutions aimed to address not only political issues but also social and cultural inequalities.

External actors, such as international organizations and foreign governments, also influenced the European color revolutions. Their support, both overt and covert, provided resources and legitimacy to student movements, amplifying their demands and increasing their impact.

Comparative analysis of the European color revolutions reveals the diverse approaches and outcomes in different countries. Each revolution had its unique characteristics, shaped by historical, cultural, and political factors. However, the role of youth and student movements remained a common thread, highlighting their agency in driving political change.

Environmental activism and sustainability were also significant aspects of the European color revolutions. Students raised awareness about the importance of environmental issues and demanded policies that prioritize sustainability and ecological responsibility.

Media coverage and propaganda during the European color revolutions played a critical role in shaping public opinion and influencing the outcome of these movements. Both state-controlled and independent media sources were utilized to disseminate information, challenge narratives, and expose government repression.

The legacy and long-term effects of the European color revolutions on European politics are still unfolding. These movements challenged the traditional power structures, inspired a new generation of activists, and paved the way for further political and social transformations. They serve as a reminder of the power of collective action and the potential for change when students and citizens demand a more democratic and just society.

Youth Engagement and the Digital Generation

The European color revolutions witnessed a significant level of youth engagement, largely driven by the digital generation. This subchapter explores the profound impact of technology and social media on the participation and mobilization of young people during this transformative period in European history.

The role of social media in the European color revolutions cannot be underestimated. Platforms such as Facebook, Twitter, and YouTube provided a space for the exchange of ideas, organization of protests, and dissemination of information. These digital tools helped to bridge geographical divides, enabling activists from different countries to connect and learn from each other's experiences. The speed and reach of social media played a crucial role in mobilizing large numbers of young people, who used these platforms to express their dissatisfaction with the prevailing political and social systems.

Artistic expressions and cultural movements also played a vital role in the European color revolutions. The digital generation, equipped with smartphones and cameras, captured powerful images and videos that became symbols of resistance and solidarity. Artistic movements, such as street art and graffiti, emerged as powerful forms of protest, challenging the established order and amplifying the voices of the youth.

The impact of economic factors on the European color revolutions cannot be ignored either. The digital generation, facing high youth unemployment rates and economic uncertainty, found themselves at the forefront of the protests. Their demands for economic justice and equality resonated with many others who were also struggling in a rapidly changing global economy.

Gender dynamics and feminism within the European color revolutions were also significant. The digital generation embraced feminist principles and advocated for gender equality. Women played a crucial role in leading and organizing protests, challenging traditional gender roles, and demanding equal representation in political decision-making processes.

The influence of external actors on the European color revolutions was evident, as support and solidarity came from international organizations, non-governmental organizations, and other countries. The digital generation utilized these connections to build networks and gain support for their causes.

In conclusion, the role of youth and student movements in the European color revolutions cannot be overstated. Their engagement was shaped by the digital generation, utilizing social media, artistic expressions, and cultural movements to challenge the status quo. Their demands for change in economic, gender, and political spheres reverberated throughout Europe, leaving a lasting impact on European politics and society.

Student Protests and University Reform

The European color revolutions of the early 21st century were marked by significant participation from student movements and their demands for university reform. These protests played a crucial role in shaping the course of these revolutions and their long-term effects on European politics. This subchapter will delve into the role of student protests in the European color revolutions, the demands put forth by these movements, and the subsequent university reforms that were implemented.

Student movements were at the forefront of the European color revolutions, utilizing social media platforms to mobilize and organize mass protests. Their demands were centered around issues such as academic freedom, democratization of universities, and the removal of corrupt university officials. These protests were often characterized by their artistic expressions and cultural movements, with students using music, graffiti, and performance art to convey their discontent and push for change.

The impact of economic factors on the European color revolutions cannot be overlooked. Students, burdened by rising tuition fees and limited job prospects, saw these protests as an opportunity to voice their grievances against the economic inequalities prevalent in their societies. The student movements also played a crucial role in highlighting the gender dynamics and advocating for feminism within the European color revolutions, demanding equal representation and opportunities for women within the movement and society at large.

External actors also had a significant influence on the European color revolutions, with various organizations and countries supporting these movements financially and politically. This subchapter will analyze the role of external actors and their motivations behind supporting the student movements.

Furthermore, a comparative analysis of the European color revolutions in different countries will be conducted, highlighting the similarities and differences in the role of student movements and university reforms. The subchapter will also explore the impact of environmental activism and sustainability within the European color revolutions, as students increasingly focused on issues of climate change and ecological sustainability.

The media coverage and propaganda during the European color revolutions will be examined, shedding light on the narratives constructed by both state-controlled and independent media outlets. Lastly, the subchapter will explore the legacy and long-term effects of the European color revolutions on European politics, analyzing how the demands of student movements and subsequent university reforms have shaped the political landscape of European countries.

In conclusion, student protests and university reform were integral components of the European color revolutions. These movements brought attention to issues of academic freedom, economic inequality, gender dynamics, and environmental sustainability. By analyzing the role of student movements, their demands, and the subsequent university reforms, this subchapter aims to provide historians with a comprehensive understanding of the impact of these protests on European politics.

Youth Political Organizations and Their Influence

The European color revolutions witnessed a remarkable surge in youth political organizations, which played a pivotal role in shaping the outcomes of these transformative movements. This subchapter aims to explore the influence of these organizations, shedding light on their strategies, impact, and contributions to the broader context of the European color revolutions.

Throughout history, young people have been at the forefront of political change, and the European color revolutions were no exception. Fueled by a combination of grievances, aspirations, and the opportunities presented by social media, young activists formed numerous organizations to channel their energy and mobilize like-minded individuals. These organizations provided a platform for young people to voice their concerns, articulate their demands, and organize protests and demonstrations.

One of the key factors that made youth political organizations influential in the European color revolutions was their adeptness in utilizing social media platforms. Harnessing the power of Facebook, Twitter, and other emerging platforms, these organizations were able to disseminate information, mobilize supporters, and coordinate actions. Their ability to quickly spread messages and rally support played a significant role in galvanizing larger segments of society and challenging the established political order.

Another crucial aspect of the influence of youth political organizations was their emphasis on artistic expressions and cultural movements. Recognizing the power of art and culture in mobilizing public sentiment, these organizations utilized music, street art, and other forms of creative expression to engage and inspire the masses. By intertwining art and political activism, they created a powerful narrative that resonated with the aspirations of the wider population.

Furthermore, youth political organizations played a crucial role in advocating for gender dynamics and feminism within the European color revolutions. Recognizing the need for inclusivity and equal representation, these organizations actively promoted gender equality and women's rights. Their efforts helped challenge traditional gender norms and ensured the active participation of women in the political process.

It is also important to acknowledge the influence of external actors on the European color revolutions. Youth political organizations often sought support and collaboration with international organizations, NGOs, and foreign governments sympathetic to their cause. The assistance provided by these external actors, both material and moral, further empowered the youth organizations and lent credibility to their demands.

In summary, youth political organizations played a vital role in the European color revolutions, leveraging social media, artistic expressions, and alliances with external actors to influence the course of events. Their ability to mobilize and inspire a wider segment of society, advocate for gender equality, and utilize innovative strategies made them a force to be reckoned with. The legacy and long-term effects of their contributions continue to shape European politics to this day.

Chapter 8: Environmental Activism and Sustainability in the European Color Revolutions

Environmental Concerns as a Catalyst for Protest

In the realm of social movements and political revolutions, one cannot underestimate the role of environmental concerns as a catalyst for protest. The European color revolutions, which swept across various countries in the early 21st century, were no exception. This subchapter examines the influence of environmental activism and sustainability on these revolutions, shedding light on the pivotal role played by environmental concerns in shaping the direction and outcomes of these transformative movements.

As the world grappled with the pressing challenges of climate change, deforestation, pollution, and resource depletion, European citizens became increasingly aware of the dire need for environmental preservation and sustainable practices. This awareness manifested itself in various forms during the color revolutions, ranging from mass protests against environmentally destructive policies to innovative grassroots initiatives promoting sustainable living and renewable energy.

One notable example of environmental activism during the European color revolutions was the movement against fracking. In countries like Poland and Romania, citizens mobilized against the extraction of shale gas through hydraulic fracturing, due to concerns over water contamination and environmental degradation. Their protests not only highlighted the detrimental impact of fracking on local ecosystems but also called for a shift towards cleaner and more sustainable energy alternatives.

Furthermore, environmental concerns also intersected with other social issues, such as economic factors and gender dynamics. The pursuit of sustainable development was seen as a means to address both environmental degradation and socio-economic inequalities. Activists advocated for green jobs, renewable energy infrastructure, and equitable distribution of resources, thereby linking environmental sustainability with economic justice.

Additionally, gender dynamics within the color revolutions were also influenced by environmental concerns. Women played a significant role in environmental activism, as they often bore the brunt of environmental degradation in their communities. Feminist movements within the color revolutions not only fought for gender equality but also sought to address the disproportionate impact of environmental problems on women.

In conclusion, environmental concerns acted as a critical catalyst for protest during the European color revolutions. From anti-fracking movements to the intersection of environmental sustainability with economic justice and gender dynamics, environmental activism played a pivotal role in shaping the direction and outcomes of these transformative movements. By understanding the influence of environmental concerns, we can gain valuable insights into the complex dynamics of social change and the long-term effects of the color revolutions on European politics.

Green Movements and Demands for Sustainable Policies

The European color revolutions of the late 20th and early 21st centuries were not only characterized by demands for political change and democratic reforms but also marked by a strong undercurrent of environmental activism and calls for sustainable policies. This subchapter explores the role of green movements within these revolutions and their demands for a more environmentally conscious society.

One of the key factors that fueled the green movements during the European color revolutions was the increasing awareness of the environmental challenges facing Europe and the world. Issues such as climate change, pollution, deforestation, and resource depletion had become pressing concerns, and activists saw the revolutions as an opportunity to address these issues and push for change.

Social media played a crucial role in mobilizing and organizing the green movements. Platforms like Facebook and Twitter allowed activists to spread information, coordinate protests, and connect with like-minded individuals across national borders. The power of social media in shaping public opinion and exerting pressure on governments cannot be underestimated, and the green movements made effective use of these tools to amplify their message.

Artistic expressions and cultural movements also played a significant role in promoting environmentalism during the European color revolutions. Artists used their creativity to raise awareness about environmental issues through various forms of media, including music, visual arts, and performance. These artistic expressions not only influenced public opinion but also provided a platform for activists to express their demands for sustainable policies.

The green movements also highlighted the impact of economic factors on the environment and called for a transition to a more sustainable and green economy. They criticized the overreliance on fossil fuels, advocated for renewable energy sources, and demanded stricter regulations to protect the environment. These demands were often met with resistance from vested interests in the energy and manufacturing sectors, but the green movements persisted, pushing for a more sustainable approach to economic development.

Furthermore, the green movements within the European color revolutions were not limited to environmental concerns alone. They recognized the interconnectedness of environmental issues with social justice, gender equality, and human rights. Feminist activists within the green movements highlighted the disproportionate impact of environmental degradation on women and called for gender-responsive policies. They emphasized the importance of including diverse voices and perspectives in the decision-making processes to ensure a more inclusive and sustainable future.

In conclusion, the green movements and demands for sustainable policies were an integral part of the European color revolutions. These movements harnessed the power of social media, utilized artistic expressions, and highlighted the impact of economic factors on the environment. They called for a transition to a more sustainable and green economy and recognized the interconnectedness of environmental issues with social justice and human rights. The legacy of these movements continues to shape European politics, with a greater emphasis on sustainability and environmental consciousness.

Climate Change and the Fight for Environmental Justice

Climate change is a global issue that has far-reaching consequences for our planet and its inhabitants. In recent years, the European color revolutions have highlighted the importance of addressing climate change and fighting for environmental justice. This subchapter explores the intersection of climate change and the European color revolutions, shedding light on the role of social media, artistic expressions, economic factors, gender dynamics, external actors, youth and student movements, environmental activism, media coverage, and the long-term effects on European politics.

The European color revolutions were marked by widespread protests and social movements that sought political change and democratic reforms. However, these revolutions were not limited to political demands alone. Many participants recognized the urgent need to address environmental issues, particularly climate change. Social media played a crucial role in mobilizing individuals and raising awareness about the impact of climate change. Platforms like Facebook, Twitter, and Instagram allowed activists to connect, organize, and share information, amplifying their message and reaching a wider audience.

Artistic expressions and cultural movements also played a significant role in the European color revolutions' fight for environmental justice. Artists used their creativity to raise awareness about climate change, creating powerful images, music, and performances that captured the attention of the public. These artistic expressions not only conveyed the urgency of the issue but also fostered a sense of unity and solidarity among activists.

Economic factors also played a crucial role in the European color revolutions and their fight for environmental justice. Economic inequalities and the unequal distribution of resources were major grievances of the protesters. Activists recognized that addressing climate change required a fundamental restructuring of economic systems and a transition towards sustainable practices. They demanded that governments prioritize environmental sustainability and invest in renewable energy sources, green technologies, and sustainable development projects.

Gender dynamics and feminism were also important aspects of the European color revolutions' fight for environmental justice. Women played a significant role in these movements, advocating for gender equality and highlighting the disproportionate impact of climate change on marginalized communities, including women and children. Feminist activists called for intersectional approaches to climate justice, recognizing that gender, race, class, and other social factors intersect with environmental issues.

External actors, such as international organizations, NGOs, and foreign governments, also influenced the European color revolutions' fight for environmental justice. These actors provided financial and technical support to activists and helped raise awareness about climate change on a global scale. Their involvement brought international attention to the issue and put pressure on governments to take action.

Overall, the European color revolutions were not just about political change but also about addressing the urgent challenges posed by climate change. Activists recognized that environmental justice was an integral part of their struggle for a more democratic and equitable society. The impact of social media, artistic expressions, economic factors, gender dynamics, external actors, and youth and student movements in the fight for environmental justice shaped the narrative of the European color revolutions and left a lasting legacy on European politics. The long-term effects of these revolutions continue to shape policy debates and political discourse around climate change in Europe and beyond.

Balancing Economic Growth and Environmental Protection

In the midst of the European color revolutions, a crucial aspect that often gets overlooked is the delicate balance between economic growth and environmental protection. These revolutions, fueled by the desire for political change and social justice, have brought to the forefront the need to address sustainable development and ecological concerns.

The role of social media in the European color revolutions cannot be understated. Platforms such as Facebook, Twitter, and Instagram played a pivotal role in mobilizing the masses and spreading awareness about the environmental challenges faced by these nations. Activists utilized these platforms to raise their voices against unsustainable practices and demand more responsible economic policies.

Artistic expressions and cultural movements also played a significant role in the European color revolutions. Artists used their creative talents to highlight the detrimental impact of economic growth on the environment. Through paintings, sculptures, and performances, they conveyed the urgent need for a more sustainable approach to economic development.

The impact of economic factors on the European color revolutions cannot be ignored. While economic growth is crucial for societal progress, the revolutions demonstrated that it should not come at the expense of the environment. Activists and environmentalists demanded policies that promote sustainable industries, renewable energy sources, and responsible resource management.

Gender dynamics and feminism within the European color revolutions also played a notable role. Women were at the forefront of the environmental movement, advocating for a more inclusive and sustainable future. They challenged traditional gender roles and called for equal representation in decision-making processes regarding economic growth and environmental protection.

External actors, such as international organizations and neighboring countries, exerted influence on the European color revolutions. They provided financial and technical support to promote sustainable development and environmental protection. Additionally, they played a crucial role in fostering regional cooperation and knowledge sharing, enabling countries to learn from each other's experiences and implement best practices.

Environmental activism and sustainability were intrinsic to the European color revolutions. Activists and civil society organizations tirelessly fought for the preservation of natural resources, biodiversity, and the reduction of carbon emissions. Their efforts helped shape policies that integrated environmental considerations into economic decision-making processes.

Media coverage and propaganda during the European color revolutions played a dual role. While some media outlets propagated the government's narrative, others provided a platform for environmental activists and their demands for sustainable economic development. The media played a crucial role in shaping public opinion and influencing policy decisions.

The legacy and long-term effects of the European color revolutions on European politics are still unfolding. However, one thing is clear: the importance of balancing economic growth and environmental protection has been firmly established. These revolutions have sparked a paradigm shift, pushing governments to adopt more sustainable policies and prioritize the protection of the environment for future generations. The European color revolutions have set a precedent for the rest of the world, highlighting the need for sustainable development that takes into account both economic growth and environmental protection.

Chapter 9: Media Coverage and Propaganda during the European Color Revolutions

Media's Role in Shaping Public Opinion

The role of the media in shaping public opinion cannot be underestimated, especially in the context of the European color revolutions. Throughout these revolutions, the media played a vital role in disseminating information, influencing public sentiment, and mobilizing the masses. This subchapter will examine the various ways in which media outlets, both traditional and social, contributed to the success and impact of the European color revolutions.

One of the most significant contributions of the media was its ability to provide real-time coverage of the protests, allowing the public to witness the events as they unfolded. Traditional media outlets, such as newspapers and television stations, played a crucial role in this regard. They provided extensive coverage of the protests, documenting the grievances of the demonstrators and exposing the corruption and authoritarianism prevalent in the regimes.

In addition to traditional media, social media platforms emerged as powerful tools for mobilization and organization during the European color revolutions. Platforms like Facebook, Twitter, and YouTube allowed protesters to share information, coordinate actions, and reach a wider audience beyond their immediate physical surroundings. Social media empowered individuals to become citizen journalists, bypassing traditional gatekeepers and providing alternative narratives to counter government propaganda.

Furthermore, the media played a significant role in shaping public opinion by highlighting the human rights abuses and injustices perpetrated by the ruling regimes. By amplifying the voices of protesters and showcasing their stories of oppression, the media garnered sympathy and support for the revolutions both domestically and internationally. This coverage helped to legitimize the demands of the protesters and delegitimize the authoritarian regimes.

However, it is important to acknowledge that the media's role was not without its challenges and shortcomings. Governments and ruling elites often resorted to propaganda and disinformation campaigns to discredit the protesters and manipulate public opinion. Media outlets that were sympathetic to the regimes also played a part in spreading false narratives and undermining the legitimacy of the movements.

In conclusion, the media's role in shaping public opinion during the European color revolutions was pivotal. Whether through traditional outlets or social media platforms, the media provided a platform for the voices of dissent to be heard and amplified. By exposing the injustices and corruption of the ruling regimes, the media played a crucial role in mobilizing public support for the revolutions. However, the media's influence was not without its challenges, as governments and ruling elites sought to undermine the credibility of the movements. Understanding the media's role in shaping public opinion during these revolutions is essential for historians seeking to analyze the long-term effects and legacy of these transformative events in European politics.

State-Controlled Media and Propaganda

In the turbulent landscape of the European color revolutions, the role of state-controlled media and propaganda cannot be overstated. This subchapter will delve into the manipulative tactics employed by governments to shape public opinion and control the narrative during these revolutionary movements. By exploring the various methods of media control and propaganda, we can gain a deeper understanding of the challenges faced by activists and the impact of these tactics on the outcomes of the revolutions.

State-controlled media, often serving as a mouthpiece for the ruling regime, played a crucial role in disseminating propaganda and suppressing dissent. Governments utilized their control over television, radio, and print media to shape public perception, demonize opposition movements, and spread disinformation. By framing the narrative in their favor, the authorities attempted to undermine the legitimacy of the protests and maintain their grip on power.

Propaganda campaigns were meticulously crafted to exploit public fears and manipulate emotions. Governments skillfully used techniques such as censorship, manipulation of news content, and the dissemination of false information to control public opinion. By portraying the opposition as dangerous or illegitimate, they sought to delegitimize the revolutionary movements and discourage public support.

In the era of social media, governments faced new challenges in controlling the flow of information. Activists harnessed the power of digital platforms to organize, mobilize, and share information, challenging the state's monopoly on news. However, governments responded by employing tactics such as internet censorship, surveillance, and the creation of fake online personas to manipulate public discourse.

Understanding the impact of state-controlled media and propaganda is crucial to comprehending the dynamics of the European color revolutions. By suppressing dissent and manipulating public opinion, governments attempted to maintain their grip on power. However, the rise of social media and the resilience of activists posed significant challenges to these tactics.

This subchapter will critically analyze the strategies employed by governments to control the media narrative and the ways in which activists navigated these challenges. By examining case studies from various countries, we can gain insights into the effectiveness of state-controlled media and propaganda and its implications for the outcomes of the European color revolutions.

Through a comparative analysis of the role of state-controlled media and propaganda, we can uncover patterns, strategies, and lessons learned from these revolutionary movements. This examination will provide historians with a comprehensive understanding of the complex interplay between media manipulation, public opinion, and the outcomes of the European color revolutions.

Independent Journalism and Citizen Reporting

One of the most significant aspects of the European color revolutions was the emergence of independent journalism and citizen reporting as powerful tools for social change. This subchapter explores the pivotal role that these forms of media played in shaping the outcome of the revolutions, and their impact on European politics.

During the European color revolutions, social media platforms such as Facebook and Twitter became instrumental in mobilizing and organizing protests. These platforms allowed citizens to share information, coordinate actions, and disseminate news in real-time. Independent journalists and citizen reporters, armed with smartphones and cameras, captured and shared footage of protests, police brutality, and acts of resistance. This grassroots reporting served as a counter-narrative to state-controlled media, which often downplayed or distorted the events unfolding on the ground.

The role of independent journalism and citizen reporting in the European color revolutions cannot be overstated. They provided an alternative source of information, challenging the dominant narratives perpetuated by the state-controlled media. By bypassing traditional media gatekeepers, these forms of media allowed citizens to tell their own stories, amplifying voices that were often marginalized or silenced.

Furthermore, independent journalism and citizen reporting helped to expose and condemn the use of propaganda by the ruling regimes. By documenting and sharing evidence of state-sponsored violence and repression, they garnered international attention and support for the revolutionaries' cause. This international solidarity, fueled by the power of independent journalism and citizen reporting, put pressure on European governments to address the demands of the protesters.

The impact of independent journalism and citizen reporting was not limited to the duration of the revolutions. Their legacy continues to shape European politics today. The revolutions highlighted the importance of a free and independent press, leading to reforms in media regulations and increased protection for journalists. Additionally, the events of the European color revolutions inspired a new generation of journalists and activists to pursue careers in independent media, ensuring that the principles of transparency and accountability remain at the forefront of European discourse.

In conclusion, independent journalism and citizen reporting played a crucial role in the European color revolutions. By providing alternative narratives, exposing propaganda, and mobilizing international support, these forms of media empowered citizens and revolutionaries alike. Their impact continues to shape European politics and serves as a testament to the power of grassroots reporting in effecting social change.

Misinformation and Disinformation Campaigns

The subchapter on "Misinformation and Disinformation Campaigns" delves into one of the most critical aspects of the European color revolutions. This chapter aims to provide historians with a comprehensive understanding of the role played by misinformation and disinformation campaigns in shaping the course and outcomes of these revolutions.

Throughout the European color revolutions, social media emerged as a powerful tool for mobilization and organizing. However, it also became a breeding ground for the dissemination of false and misleading information. This subchapter explores the various ways in which social media platforms were exploited to spread misinformation and disinformation during these revolutions. By analyzing specific incidents and case studies, historians can gain insights into the techniques employed, the impact on public opinion, and the subsequent actions taken by the revolutionaries.

In addition to social media, artistic expressions and cultural movements played a significant role in the European color revolutions. This subchapter examines how misinformation and disinformation were propagated through artistic mediums, such as music, street art, and performances. By studying these artistic expressions, historians can uncover the narratives and ideologies that were intentionally disseminated to manipulate public sentiment.

Furthermore, economic factors played a crucial role in the European color revolutions. This subchapter investigates the ways in which misinformation and disinformation campaigns were employed to exploit economic grievances and incite unrest. By understanding the intersection between economic factors and misinformation, historians can analyze the impact on the trajectory and outcomes of these revolutions.

The subchapter also delves into the gender dynamics and feminism within the European color revolutions. It explores how misinformation and disinformation campaigns targeted women's rights movements, attempting to undermine their credibility and marginalize their demands. By examining these campaigns, historians can shed light on the challenges faced by feminist movements and the strategies employed to counteract misinformation.

Moreover, the influence of external actors on the European color revolutions is a crucial aspect to be explored. This subchapter investigates how misinformation and disinformation campaigns were orchestrated by foreign entities to manipulate public opinion and advance their own interests. Through a comparative analysis, historians can discern the similarities and differences in the tactics employed by external actors in different countries.

Overall, the subchapter on "Misinformation and Disinformation Campaigns" provides historians with a nuanced understanding of the role played by misinformation and disinformation in the European color revolutions. By analyzing the impact of social media, artistic expressions, economic factors, gender dynamics, external actors, and more, historians can uncover the complex web of manipulation that shaped these historic events. This knowledge serves as a foundation for future research and a cautionary tale about the power of information in influencing political movements.

Chapter 10: The Legacy and Long-Term Effects of the European Color Revolutions on European Politics

Democratization and Political System Changes

The European color revolutions marked a significant turning point in the history of the continent, bringing about profound democratization and political system changes. These revolutions, characterized by their peaceful nature and reliance on social movements rather than armed conflict, had far-reaching implications for European politics. This subchapter explores the transformative impact of these revolutions on the political landscape and the resulting changes in the democratization process.

One of the key catalysts for the success of the European color revolutions was the role of social media. The subchapter delves into how platforms such as Facebook, Twitter, and YouTube played a pivotal role in mobilizing and organizing citizens, facilitating the rapid dissemination of information and ideas. It examines the ways in which social media empowered grassroots movements and enabled them to challenge oppressive regimes.

Artistic expressions and cultural movements also played a significant role in the European color revolutions. The subchapter explores how artists and cultural activists used their creative platforms to challenge the status quo, express dissent, and inspire collective action. It examines the impact of artistic expressions and cultural movements on the mobilization and consciousness of the people, highlighting their contribution to the democratization process.

Furthermore, the subchapter investigates the influence of economic factors on the European color revolutions. It examines the socio-economic grievances that fueled these revolutions, such as corruption, unemployment, and income inequality. It also analyzes how economic factors interacted with political demands, shaping the trajectory of the movements and their demands for systemic change.

Gender dynamics and feminism played a significant role in the European color revolutions, and the subchapter explores the impact of these movements on gender equality and women's empowerment. It discusses how women played a pivotal role in these revolutions and analyzes the challenges they faced in their pursuit of political change.

The subchapter also examines the influence of external actors on the European color revolutions. It explores the role of international organizations, foreign governments, and non-state actors in supporting or undermining these movements, shedding light on the complexities of external intervention in democratization processes.

To provide a comprehensive analysis, the subchapter offers a comparative analysis of the European color revolutions in different countries. It explores the similarities and differences in the causes, dynamics, and outcomes of these revolutions, highlighting the contextual factors that shaped their trajectories.

Additionally, the subchapter explores the role of youth and student movements in the European color revolutions, examining how young people became key agents of change and highlighting their demands for political reform.

Environmental activism and sustainability were also prominent themes in the European color revolutions. The subchapter explores how environmental concerns and sustainability became intertwined with political demands, reflecting a growing awareness of the interconnections between democracy, social justice, and environmental protection.

Media coverage and propaganda during the European color revolutions are also analyzed in the subchapter. It examines the role of state-controlled media, independent journalism, and foreign media in shaping public opinion and influencing the outcomes of these revolutions.

Finally, the subchapter explores the legacy and long-term effects of the European color revolutions on European politics. It examines how these revolutions reshaped political institutions, influenced policy-making processes, and transformed the relationship between citizens and the state.

In conclusion, this subchapter provides a comprehensive analysis of the democratization and political system changes brought about by the European color revolutions. It explores the role of social media, artistic expressions, economic factors, gender dynamics, external actors, youth and student movements, environmental activism, media coverage, and the long-term effects of these revolutions on European politics. By examining these various dimensions, the subchapter offers historians a deeper understanding of the transformative power of these revolutions and their enduring impact on European society.

The Rise of Populist Movements in Europe

Introduction:

In recent years, Europe has witnessed the emergence and rapid rise of populist movements across the continent. These movements, characterized by their anti-establishment rhetoric and nationalist ideologies, have challenged the traditional political landscape and sparked debates about the future of European politics. This subchapter aims to explore the factors behind the rise of populist movements in Europe, their impact on the European color revolutions, and the long-term effects on European politics.

Factors contributing to the rise of populist movements:

Populist movements in Europe have been fueled by a variety of factors, including economic instability, cultural anxieties, and the perceived erosion of national sovereignty. The impact of economic factors, such as income inequality and job insecurity, cannot be underestimated. These economic grievances have created fertile ground for populist leaders who promise to protect the interests of the working class and restore economic prosperity.

Additionally, the role of social media in the rise of populist movements cannot be overlooked. Platforms like Facebook, Twitter, and YouTube have provided a powerful tool for populist leaders to bypass traditional media channels and directly communicate with their supporters. This subchapter will examine the role of social media in shaping the narrative and mobilizing support for populist movements during the European color revolutions.

The impact of populist movements on the European color revolutions:

Populist movements have had a significant impact on the European color revolutions, both as catalysts for change and as potential threats to democratic norms. While populist movements have successfully mobilized large segments of the population and challenged the status quo, their nationalist and anti-immigrant ideologies have also raised concerns about the erosion of democratic values and the rise of authoritarianism.

Comparative analysis of populist movements in different countries:

This subchapter will provide a comparative analysis of populist movements in different European countries, including France, Italy, Hungary, and the United Kingdom. By examining the similarities and differences between these movements, historians can gain a deeper understanding of the factors that have contributed to their rise and the unique challenges they have posed to European politics.

Conclusion:

The rise of populist movements in Europe has had profound implications for the European color revolutions and the future of European politics. By examining the factors behind their rise, their impact on the revolutions, and the long-term effects on European politics, historians can gain valuable insights into this transformative period in European history. It is essential to understand the role of social media, the influence of external actors, and the dynamics of gender, youth, and environmental activism to fully grasp the complexities of the European color revolutions and their lasting legacy.

Lessons Learned and Applied in Subsequent Protests

As historians delve into the rich tapestry of the European Color Revolutions, it becomes evident that these movements were not isolated events but rather a catalyst for a wave of change across the continent. Subsequent protests drew on the lessons learned from these revolutions, shaping the course of European history in various domains. From the role of social media to the impact of economic factors, gender dynamics, and external influences, the European Color Revolutions have left an indelible mark on the fabric of European society.

One of the most significant lessons learned from these revolutions was the power of social media in mobilizing and organizing large-scale protests. The use of platforms such as Facebook, Twitter, and YouTube allowed activists to connect, share information, and coordinate actions in real-time. This realization has since influenced subsequent protests, leading to the emergence of new social movements that utilize social media as a primary tool for mobilization.

Artistic expressions and cultural movements also played a pivotal role in the European Color Revolutions. The power of music, street art, and other creative forms of expression were harnessed to convey messages of dissent and unity. These artistic expressions resonated deeply with the public, leading to increased participation and solidarity. As a result, subsequent protests have incorporated artistic elements to amplify their message and engage a wider audience.

The impact of economic factors on the European Color Revolutions cannot be understated. The revolutions were driven, in part, by economic grievances, including corruption, inequality, and unemployment. The subsequent protests have learned from these economic factors, focusing their demands on issues of economic justice, fair distribution of wealth, and transparency in governance.

Gender dynamics and feminism emerged as significant themes within the European Color Revolutions. Women played a prominent role in these movements, challenging patriarchal norms and advocating for gender equality. This has had a lasting impact on subsequent protests, with feminist movements gaining momentum and demanding equal rights and representation.

The influence of external actors on the European Color Revolutions was another crucial lesson learned. The involvement of international organizations, foreign governments, and non-state actors shaped the outcomes of these revolutions. Subsequent protests have taken note of this influence, adopting strategies to counter external interference and safeguard their movements' autonomy.

Comparative analysis of the European Color Revolutions in different countries has allowed historians to identify common patterns and unique characteristics. This analysis has provided valuable insights into the factors that contribute to the success or failure of such movements, aiding subsequent protests in their strategic planning and decision-making.

The role of youth and student movements in the European Color Revolutions cannot be overlooked. Young people played a vital role in mobilizing and organizing protests, bringing fresh perspectives and energy to the forefront. Subsequent protests have recognized the power of youth and student movements, actively involving them in their campaigns and leveraging their passion for change.

Environmental activism and sustainability have also become central themes in subsequent protests. The European Color Revolutions highlighted the interconnectedness of social and environmental issues, inspiring a new wave of environmental activism that seeks to address climate change, protect natural resources, and promote sustainable practices.

Media coverage and propaganda during the European Color Revolutions were critical factors that shaped public opinion and the outcomes of these movements. Lessons learned from the manipulation of information and the spread of propaganda have led subsequent protests to employ media strategies that counter misinformation and ensure accurate representation of their objectives.

Lastly, the legacy and long-term effects of the European Color Revolutions on European politics are of utmost significance. These revolutions challenged the status quo, leading to political transformations, reforms, and new avenues for citizen participation. Subsequent protests have aimed to build upon this legacy, striving for lasting change and influencing the political landscape in Europe.

In conclusion, the European Color Revolutions have left a profound impact on various aspects of European society. Lessons learned from these revolutions have been applied in subsequent protests, shaping the role of social media, artistic expressions, economic factors, gender dynamics, external influences, comparative analysis, youth movements, environmental activism, media coverage, and the long-term effects on European politics. As historians, it is essential to explore these lessons to gain a comprehensive understanding of the European Color Revolutions and their enduring influence.

A New Era of Activism and Civic Engagement

The European Color Revolutions marked a turning point in the history of activism and civic engagement in Europe. These revolutions, which took place in various countries across the continent, were characterized by widespread public protests and calls for political change. What made these revolutions unique was the role of social media, artistic expressions, economic factors, gender dynamics, external actors, youth and student movements, environmental activism, media coverage, and the long-term effects on European politics.

Social media played a crucial role in mobilizing and organizing the masses during the European Color Revolutions. Platforms such as Facebook and Twitter allowed activists to disseminate information quickly and efficiently, creating a sense of unity and solidarity among protesters. The use of hashtags and online campaigns helped to amplify their messages and reach a wider audience than ever before.

Artistic expressions and cultural movements also played a significant role in the European Color Revolutions. Artists, musicians, and writers used their creative talents to express dissent and inspire change. Street art, graffiti, and performances became powerful symbols of resistance, creating a visual language that resonated with the public and challenged the status quo.

Economic factors were another driving force behind these revolutions. High unemployment rates, income inequality, and corruption fueled public discontent and frustration. The economic hardships faced by ordinary citizens became a rallying point for protesters, who demanded greater economic opportunities and fairness.

Gender dynamics and feminism within the European Color Revolutions were also noteworthy. Women played a prominent role in these movements, challenging traditional gender roles and advocating for gender equality. Feminist groups and activists fought for women's rights and empowerment, contributing to a more inclusive and diverse movement.

The influence of external actors on the European Color Revolutions cannot be ignored. International organizations, such as the European Union and NATO, provided support and guidance to activists, offering a platform for their voices to be heard on the global stage. External actors also played a role in shaping the outcome of these revolutions, influencing the direction of political change.

The role of youth and student movements in the European Color Revolutions was pivotal. Young people, disillusioned with the existing political order, took to the streets to demand a better future. Their energy, passion, and innovative tactics injected new life into the movements, challenging traditional power structures.

Environmental activism and sustainability also emerged as significant themes during the European Color Revolutions. Activists called for greater environmental protection, sustainable development, and climate justice. These demands reflected a growing awareness of the need for a more sustainable and environmentally responsible society.

Media coverage and propaganda during the European Color Revolutions played a crucial role in shaping public opinion. Mainstream media outlets, as well as alternative media platforms, provided coverage of the events, amplifying the voices of activists and exposing government repression. However, propaganda and disinformation were also used to manipulate public perception and undermine the legitimacy of the protests.

Finally, the legacy and long-term effects of the European Color Revolutions on European politics are still being felt today. These revolutions sparked a wave of political change across the continent, leading to the downfall of authoritarian regimes and the rise of more democratic and accountable governments. The protests also inspired a new generation of activists and engaged citizens, who continue to fight for social justice and political reform.

In conclusion, the European Color Revolutions ushered in a new era of activism and civic engagement in Europe. The role of social media, artistic expressions, economic factors, gender dynamics, external actors, youth and student movements, environmental activism, media coverage, and the long-term effects on European politics were all instrumental in shaping the course of these revolutions. By examining these various aspects, historians can gain a deeper understanding of the complexities and dynamics of this transformative period in European history.

As historians delve into the intricate tapestry of the European color revolutions, it becomes evident that a comprehensive understanding of this transformative period requires a nuanced exploration of various factors at play. This subchapter serves as a reminder that the outlined structure of this book is flexible and subject to modification based on the author's unique research and findings.

The role of social media in the European color revolutions remains a captivating subject of study. Social media platforms such as Facebook and Twitter played a pivotal role in mobilizing and organizing protesters, reshaping the dynamics of public discourse, and challenging traditional power structures. By examining the impact of these platforms on the revolutions, historians can gain valuable insights into the transformative potential of digital activism.

Artistic expressions and cultural movements during the European color revolutions provide another captivating lens through which to view this period of change. From street art to music festivals, creative forms of dissent and cultural expression played an integral role in shaping the collective identity and aspirations of the protesters. By analyzing these artistic expressions, historians can uncover the complex interplay between politics and culture during this time.

The impact of economic factors on the European color revolutions cannot be understated. Rising economic inequality, corruption, and austerity measures fueled public discontent and served as catalysts for these revolutions. By examining the economic grievances and demands of the protesters, historians can shed light on the intricate relationship between economics and political change.

Gender dynamics and feminism within the European color revolutions offer a fascinating perspective on the role of women in these movements. Women played crucial roles as leaders, organizers, and activists, challenging patriarchal norms and advocating for gender equality. By exploring the experiences of women during this period, historians can uncover the transformative power of feminist movements within the broader context of the revolutions.

The influence of external actors on the European color revolutions is a topic that demands careful analysis. Whether it be through financial support, diplomatic intervention, or covert operations, external actors had a significant impact on the outcomes of these revolutions. By examining the role of external actors, historians can unravel the intricate web of geopolitical interests that shaped the course of these revolutions.

By delving into the niches of the role of social media, artistic expressions, economic factors, gender dynamics, external actors, and other themes within the European color revolutions, historians can weave together a rich tapestry of analysis, providing invaluable insights into this transformative period and its lasting effects on European politics.